CARS

MUSTANG

Michael Bradley

mc **Marshall Cavendish**
Benchmark
New York

Marshall Cavendish Benchmark
99 White Plains Road
Tarrytown, NY 10591-5502
www.marshallcavendish.us

All Internet sites were available and accurate when sent to press.

Library of Congress Cataloging-in-Publication Data

Bradley, Michael, 1962–
Mustang / by Michael Bradley.
p. cm. — (Cars)
Includes bibliographical references and index.
ISBN 978-0-7614-2982-1
1. Mustang automobile—Juvenile literature. I. Title. II. Series.
TL215.M8B73 2009
629.222'2—dc22
2007036988

Photo research by Connie Gardner

Cover photo by © Ron Kimball Stock Photography/Ron Kimball

The photographs in this book are used by permission and through the courtesy of: *Ron Kimball/www. kimballstock.com*: back cover, 8, 14, 15, 18, 20, 28; *Alamy*: Frances Roberts, 1; Mark Scheuern, 9; Phil Talbot, 17; Jom Friedrich, 25; *Corbis*: Bettmann, 4, 11; Hulton Deutsch Collection, 6; Car Culture, 16, 24, 26; *Ford Communication Services/Ford Still Image Library*: 5, 7, 10, 12 (T); *From the Collections of the Henry Ford*: 12 (B), 23; *AP Photo*: Mary Altaffer, 13; Jason De Crow, 27; *John E. Gillmore III, Photographer*: 29.

Publisher: Michelle Bisson
Art Director: Anahid Hamparian
Series Designer: Daniel Roode

Printed in Malaysia
1 3 5 6 4 2

CONTENTS

The Mustang was a nationwide sensation as soon as it debuted in 1964. According to Ford Motor Company, more than twenty thousand orders were placed when it was unveiled at the World's Fair in New York.

He had to have it. He just had to. So, he slept—in the car.

The man from Texas had outbid a group of people for the last Mustang at the **dealership**. The car had just been introduced, and he wanted one. He needed one. So, when he was told it would take a day to make sure he had enough money in the bank to cover the check he wrote to pay for the car, he didn't take any chances. He spent the night in his new Mustang and drove off in it the next morning. If the bank had said the check was no good, he would have paid cash. Or sold his house. But he was taking the car home.

The 1965 Mustang convertible became more popular when the car appeared in the James Bond movie *Goldfinger*.

That sounds pretty crazy today, but it was just part of the Mustang mania that hit in April 1964. The car that Ford had promoted as the American **version** of an English-style sports car was a huge hit. Some people at the automaker had been afraid the hype leading up to the Mustang's **debut** would **backfire**. They remembered how everybody was excited about the Edsel in the 1950s. That didn't go well at all.

They shouldn't have worried a bit. The Mustang took off like the spirited horse for which it was named. It had good looks, plenty of power, and was just plain cool. At a time when other car companies were creating their own sporty models, like Chevrolet's Corvette and the Dodge Charger, Ford had a successful product.

The Mustang is as much a symbol of the 1960s as the Woodstock music festival.

The Indianapolis 500 selected a Ford Mustang to be the official pace car in 1964 (shown here), 1979, and 1994.

America sure took to it. *Time* and *Newsweek* magazines featured the new Mustang on their covers during the same week. Dealers sold every car they were initially given, leaving the next wave of buyers to suffer through an eight-week wait. The Indianapolis 500 chose the one-month-old Mustang as its official **pace car** in 1964, giving it even more attention. The Mustang was hot, all right.

Available with a V-6 or a V-8 engine, buyers had a choice when purchasing a 1966 Mustang: fast or faster!

And it has stayed hot for more than forty years. Sure, there were some ups and downs, like when the government ruled that cars had to have better fuel economy. That was tough. Sales were also down during the 1980s, when Ford tried to change with the times, and the Mustang lost a little of its personality. For the most part, the Mustang has been one of the country's most recognizable and desirable cars ever since its debut.

Its classic look has not only endured, it has come back by popular demand. The twenty-first-century Mustang looks more like its mid—1960s **ancestor** than anything else. People continue to buy in big numbers because the Mustang has plenty of power. Whether you're cruising with the top down or prowling the streets in a coupe, you're never out of style with a Mustang.

There aren't any **stampedes** to the dealer anymore, and people aren't sleeping in the cars to make sure they get one. But Mustang has endured as one of the few true **icons** of the American road.

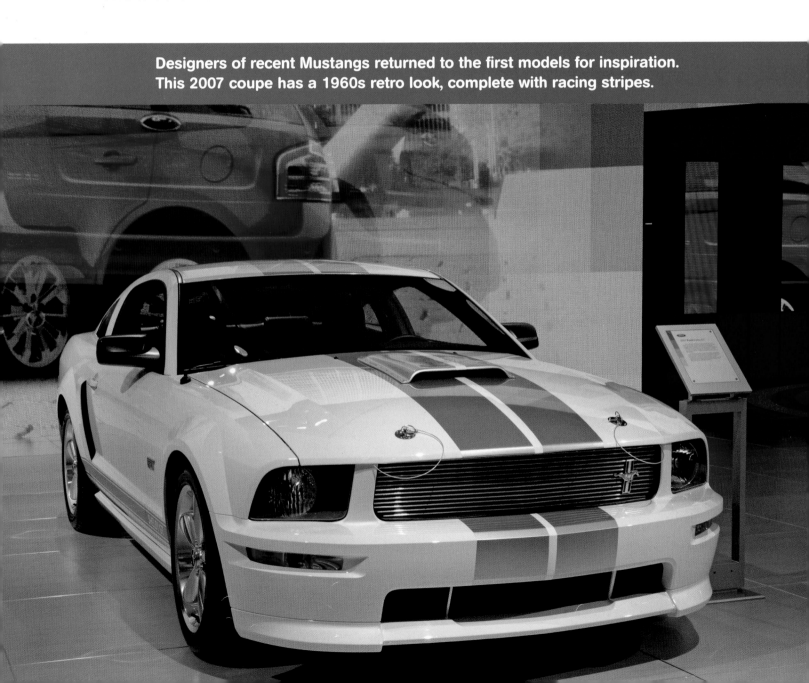

Designers of recent Mustangs returned to the first models for inspiration. This 2007 coupe has a 1960s retro look, complete with racing stripes.

The Ford Falcon convertible was the prototype for the Mustang.
In fact, before Mustang became its official name, the car was
called the Special Falcon (shown here) and the Torino.

To many who are aware of the history of the American automobile, Lee Iacocca is known as the man who helped turn Chrysler from a **bankrupt** mess into a **profit** machine. But to Mustang drivers and fans, he is the car's godfather.

In the early 1960s Ford asked Iacocca to work on the T-5 Project, also known as the Special Falcon. It was a secret **venture** in which Iacocca was asked to develop an affordable sports car. Although the early

Ford wanted to market the Mustang as a fast sports car, so they named it after the P-51 Mustang fighter plane.

A couple look at the new Ford Mustang at the 1964 World's Fair. Mustangs were not only fast and stylish, but affordable.

designs and concept cars were two-seaters with high-powered engines and convertible tops, the finished product finally emerged. As the plans moved ahead, the car was given its name, thanks to Ford executive stylist John Naijar, who was fascinated by the P-51 Mustang, a World War II fighter plane.

As the launch date of April 17, 1964, approached, Ford began the promotional **blitz** for the Mustang. Automobile writers were given information and invited to "ride and drive" sessions at which they could get behind the wheel. Select dealers were invited to a music show that introduced the car and created excitement about it. Four days before the car debuted, seventy-five auto writers were invited to the Ford tent at the World's Fair in New York. There, they were each given

In 1967 Ford produced three Mustang models: the convertible (top left), the 2+2 fastback (top right), and the hardtop.

Mustang '6

the keys to a Mustang and told to drive it back home. That generated a lot of buzz. On April 14, Ford aired commercials at 9:30 p.m. on all three major television networks (there weren't 200 channels back then!). America was ready for the Mustang.

During the 1960s Ford teamed up with famous sports-car designer Carroll Shelby to produce the Mustang Cobra line. Like most Mustangs, this 1965 Cobra features bucket seats.

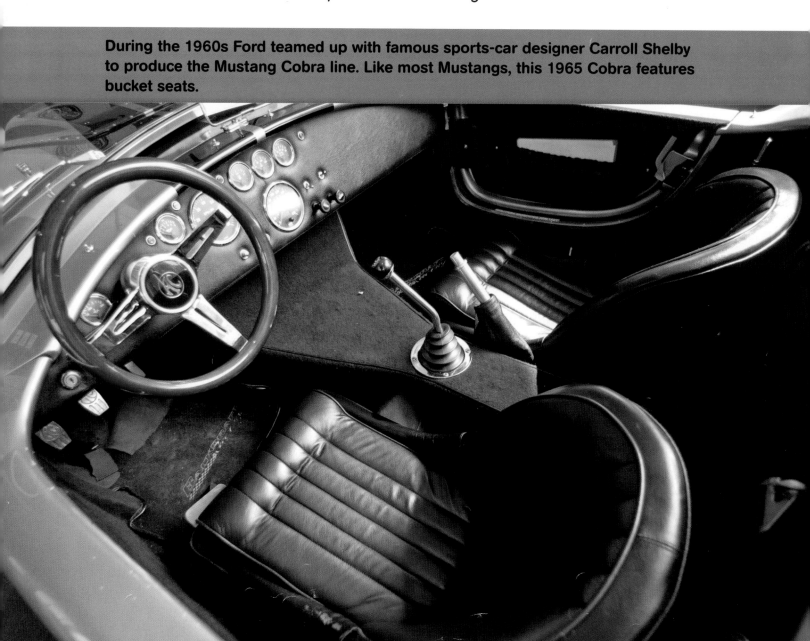

On Mustang's first weekend, more than 4 million people visited showrooms around the country, and 22,000 orders were placed. One truck driver was passing a dealership and stared at the Mustang so long that he drove through the showroom window. This was one hot car.

What caused the stir? First, of course, was the look. The Mustang had a low roof. The taillights were vertical, giving it a unique appearance from behind. Side **scallops** on the car looked like ribs or fish gills. Even better was the price. While the Chevrolet Corvette checked in at $3,800, the Mustang cost only $2,500. It was a four-seat family car that had real power and a cool, sports-car look. What else could you ask for?

Ford sure didn't have any complaints. In the first year, 417,000 people bought Mustangs, the top sales figure in automotive history. Ten months later Ford passed the one-million mark in number of car sales. On April 16, 1965, the National Council of Mustang Owners held its first "Rally Day," and 12,500 people showed up with their cars.

Ford introduced the Mustang convertible at the end of 1964, complete with a **replica** of a racing steering wheel. In 1965 the coupe was introduced, and the GT made its debut, complete with a fiery V-8 engine and dual twin **exhausts**. The **muscle car** was born. While Americans were snapping it up, Ford was building the Mustang reputation at racetracks across the country, taking home trophies and leaving other companies green with envy. The Mustang was really rolling.

And it was just getting started.

The 1967 Shelby Cobra GT500 featured a V-8 engine that pumped out 355 horsepower. It was also the first model to feature the coiled cobra logo.

The world is a blur when you're behind the wheel of a Mustang!
The 1969 Boss 429 Mustang Fastback could clock a time of
fourteen seconds for the quarter mile.

CHAPTER THREE
GROWING UP AND UP

The year was 1969, and muscle cars were popular throughout the United States. Drivers wanted something with extra power, something that could blast past just about anything else on the road, and something that looked cool. The answer was simple: the Mustang.

Four years earlier Ford had introduced the GT, a V-8 model with dual exhaust pipes and sharp side-roof vents. The car looked fast, and it moved fast. By 1969, it had brought

The Mustang Boss, like the Ford Thunderbird and the Chevrolet Corvette, was a pony car—fast and sporty. These cars later became known as muscle cars.

One look at this sleek 2003 Mustang Cobra and it's easy to see why the car is America's top-selling convertible.

out the Boss and the Mach 1, two versions of the original that were pumped up and ready to impress. The Mach 1 was pure power, giving drivers everything they wanted in a sports car.

The Boss, meanwhile, had its roots in the racing world and was designed to help Ford gain entry into the Trans-Am Series, a road-racing competition. A year later the Boss 429 hit the streets with a roar of thunder. The engine was so big that it wouldn't fit into a regular Mustang frame without some changes to the car's **suspension**. In reality, it wasn't made for the road. Ford needed a car to put an engine in for NASCAR racing, so it chose the Mustang. As a result, only 499 were made, and some consider the Boss 429 the greatest Mustang of them all, thanks to its power, wide tires, and aggressive-looking front end.

While 1970 represented the peak of Mustang's muscle flexing, it also signaled a downturn in sales. Thanks to strong efforts by competitors like Chevrolet's Camaro, Plymouth's Barracuda, and Pontiac's Firebird, Ford's sales began to dip. There were more choices out there, and though Mustang remained one of the sharpest cars around, some drivers looked elsewhere. Also, the U.S. government passed the federal Clean Air Act, which tried to cut down on the pollution produced by cars—especially by powerful cars. Mustang, with its growling V-8, had to make

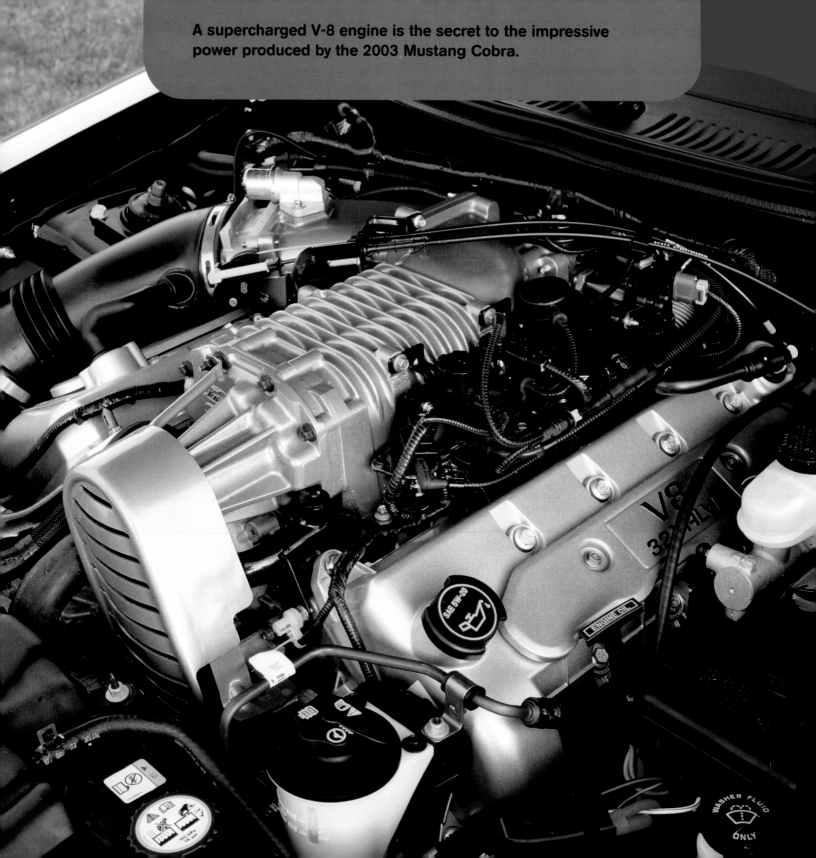

A supercharged V-8 engine is the secret to the impressive power produced by the 2003 Mustang Cobra.

some changes. So, in 1971, Ford produced its final muscle car, the Mach 1. Two years later, the last of the first **generation** of Mustangs rolled off the production line.

Drivers wanted smaller cars, in part because gas was getting more expensive. So the Mustang became more compact for 1974. It also lost its convertible top, at least for the next ten years. When the new model debuted, Ford called it "the most changed car in the industry." A year later it was even more different than its ancestors, with a half-vinyl top, **opera windows**, and a V-6 engine.

The convertible returned in 1983, and the Mustang returned to its performance roots. Even though it had to use a smaller engine and pay more attention to fuel efficiency, the Mustang could still go. As the decade rolled on, and the 1990s dawned, Mustang continued to evolve. It was low to the ground, still extremely powerful, and styled to look better than just about anything on the road.

By 2003 it was time to look back. Way back. Ford looked to the 1960s for inspiration and created a Mustang that was ready to cruise the main drag. But inside its retro frame was an updated engine that delivered plenty of twenty-first-century power and an interior that was comfortable and sleek. Mustang had come full circle with a car that looked back and looked forward.

CHAPTER FOUR
STYLE POINTS

The first version was a little too much. It had a low, wraparound windshield and a sleek front end that looked like a shark's nose. It had just two seats and a radical back window that stuck up in the air. It was incredibly cool and about twenty years too soon.

So Ford junked it.

Actually, the Mustang I Concept Car did a little racing, but it never made it to the showroom. America just wasn't ready for it.

But U.S. drivers were prepared for the first Mustang, and why not? The car was unlike anything else out there, from its triple vertical taillights to its superior handling.

The Mustang came in three versions: the coupe, the convertible, and a fastback model that featured a long rear window and **simulated** side vents just behind the doors.

That unique look was what people could count on about the Mustang from the moment it was introduced. Sure, other cars had their own personalities, but the Mustang was special. And you could see it as the years went on, and the car began its trip to the twenty-first century.

The Mustang I Concept Car was modeled after the P-51 fighter. The body was smooth, rounded, and compact, which not only looked cool, but enabled the car to go fast.

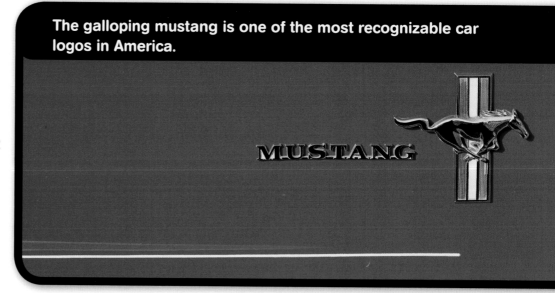

The galloping mustang is one of the most recognizable car logos in America.

A few things stayed the same, such as the classic Mustang logo, which featured a **galloping** pony set against a backdrop of red, white, and blue stripes. The pony appeared again on the front grill, announcing the car's arrival. But there were changes. The most obvious was in the car's size. Beginning in 1967, the car got larger because Americans became more interested in speed and power. The 1967 Mustang was not only larger, but also built lower to the ground, enabling it to move faster.

In 1965 the company began its five-year partnership with **legendary** sports-car designer and racer Carroll Shelby, a Texan with an eye for sharp lines and fast machines. The Shelby GT350 was born in 1965 and gave racing enthusiasts something to drive on the suburban streets. By 1967 the rocket on wheels had a 428 cubic-inch engine.

Although Mustang changed its look throughout the 1970s and 1980s, it still could make a splash. The Cobra II had stripes, spoilers, a **T-top,** and other sporty features, not to mention plenty of power. In the early 1990s, performance-car master Steve Saleen designed a Mustang that was more powerful than the ordinary showroom versions, had a suspension that improved the car's handling at high speeds, comfortable leather seats, and a convertible top. As usual, Mustang was giving its fans a little something extra.

Saleen was at it again in 2007 with the Parnelli Jones Limited Edition model. The car was named for the legendary race car driver who won the Indy 500 in 1963 and captured many other racing titles.

With a light body and a powerful engine, the 1965 Shelby GT350R was designed for the race track, not the highway.

In 1968 Ford's 428 Cobra Jet left its competition in the dust at the
Pomona, California, drag races, boasting close to 400 horsepower.

The Mustang came in only one color: Grabber Orange. It featured black striping, a rear spoiler, and special race wheels. One look and you were back in 1970. It was pretty cool.

Just like the Mustang has always been.

Parnelli Jones—winner of the 1963 Indy 500—stands next to his namesake, the retro-inspired 2007 Parnelli Jones Limited Edition Mustang.

Vital Statistics

1965 Mustang **(released in April 1964)**

Power: 278 hp
Engine Size: 289 ci/4.7L
Engine Type: V-8
Weight: 2,550 lbs. (1,159 kg)
Top Speed: 120 mph (193 km/h)
0–60 mph (0–96.5 km/h): 7.5 sec

2008 Mustang GT

Power: 300 hp
Engine Size: 281ci/4.6L
Engine Type: SOHC V-8
Weight: 3,500 lbs. (1,588 kg)
Top Speed: 143 mph (230 km/h)
0–60 mph (0–96.5 km/h): 4.5 sec

GLOSSARY

ancestor	Usually refers to a person from an earlier time, but it can also mean an earlier version of a car.
backfire	To go wrong.
bankrupt	When a person is legally declared unable to pay the money he or she owes.
blitz	A sudden attack that overwhelms an opponent.
dealership	A business that sells a product in a certain area for a larger company.
debut	The first appearance of something in public.
exhaust	A pipe through which steam, smoke, or gas travels as it leaves an engine.
gallop	To move very quickly by taking long, strong strides.
generation	A group of people or cars existing at the same point in time.
icon	A symbol of something that is highly respected.
legendary	Something that is extremely respected and with a story that has survived over many years.
muscle car	The name given to a breed of automobile in the late 1960s and early 1970s that featured a large, powerful engine and a bulky frame that was capable of traveling quickly.
opera windows	Small, rear side windows that increase visibility.
pace car	A car that leads the competing race cars through a warm-up lap, but does not take part in the race.
profit	The amount left over after costs are subtracted from money taken in by a business.
replica	A copy of something.

scallop	A curve that is made to look like a seashell.
simulated	Made to look real.
stampede	A great rush of many people or animals toward a common target.
suspension	The system of springs and other supporting devices that are part of a vehicle's frame.
T-top	An automobile roof with two removable panels on either side of a straight bar that connects the front and rear windshields.
venture	A somewhat risky undertaking, such as a new business launch.
version	One form of a product or idea.

FURTHER INFORMATION

BOOKS

Covert, Patrick. *Ultimate Mustang*. New York: DK Publishing, 2002.

Ilaria, Henry W. *Ford Mustang Anthology*. Gilroy, CA: Hi-Tech Software, 2006.

Leffingwell, Randy. *Mustang: Forty Years*. St. Paul, MN: Motorbooks, 2003.

DVD

The Complete Mustang, 40th Anniversary. America's Favorite Cars Series. Estate Films, 2004.

WEB SITES

www.fordvehicles.com/cars/mustang

www.mustangsandfords.com

www.mustangheaven.com

INDEX

About the Author

MICHAEL BRADLEY is a writer and broadcaster who lives near Philadelphia. He has written for *Sports Illustrated for Kids*, *Hoop*, *Inside Stuff*, and *Slam* magazines and is a regular contributor to Comcast SportsNet in Philadelphia.